Bread Machine Cookbook

The Ultimate Guide to Master Bread Machines, with Quick, Tasty and Stress-Free Recipes for Delicious Bakes Full of Variety

By

Poppy Green

Contents

Introduction

Baking Bread has been completely transformed thanks to the introduction of bread machines. You no longer have to spend significant time kneading, raising, and baking bread. Using a bread machine, anyone can make fresh bread only with a few basic ingredients and the push of a button. The bread will come out fresh and delicious every time. If you start in the kitchen, do not let the prospect of operating a bread maker frighten you. They are highly user-friendly and provide many different recipes for one to pick from. The bread machine is just an instrument that should not be noticed by only some who enjoy eating freshly baked bread that has just come out of the oven, regardless of their baking experience.

This book will provide an overview of the bread machine industry and instructions on using one. We will examine the many bread machines on the market and discuss how to select the most suitable model for your requirements. In addition, we will supply you with mouthwatering recipes to try and provide you with some pointers on how to make the most out of your equipment. It is the right resource for you, whether you are a busy mother who wants to prepare nutritious, handmade bread for the family or simply seeking an easier way to bake fresh bread. In any case, you will find the information you need here. We will walk you through the process step-by-step and provide you with handy tips on making the most of the new bread machine so that you can quickly start baking wonderful bread.

Why hold off, then? Begin so you may experience the pleasure of baking homemade bread and have it turn out perfectly every time. With the help of this instruction, you will be ready to bake delicious bread with a satisfying crust that your loved ones will like. Get your bread machine and all of the necessary ingredients ready because we're about to get started.

Chapter 1: Introduction to Bread Machines

Bread has a long history of consumption and is considered a necessary food in a variety of diets and traditions all over the world. In addition to serving as the foundation for a wide variety of foods, it can take anything from a straightforward loaf to a complex pastry. Bread machines are just one example of how technological advancements have made formerly simple tasks like homemade baking bread simpler.

An electronic kitchen gadget known as a bread maker can fully automate the process of creating bread, from the initial combining of the ingredients to the final kneading and baking of the dough and bread. Home bakers will find its operation straightforward and uncomplicated, and it offers a wide variety of customization options, including a selection of crust colors and loaf sizes.

When making bread with a bread machine, put the ingredients into the bread pan in the order that the maker of the bread machine specifies. After that, the machine will mix, knead, let the bread rise, and bake it, all within a few hours at most. People who have hectic lives and don't have the time to make wheat from scratch may find this an extremely helpful option.

Bread machines can be found in various forms and dimensions, but they all have certain essential components: a bread pan, a combining blade, and a heat source for baking. Some models also come equipped with a timer that enables the user to schedule the machine to begin functioning at a predetermined time, allowing the user to have freshly baked bread waiting for them when they get home after work.

Bread machines can produce a wide variety of bread, including white bread, full wheat bread, and specialty loaves that include components such as nuts, berries, and spices among their constituents. Some machines also have specialized programming for producing other baked items, such as jam, cake, and dough for pasta.

Using a bread machine removes the element of chance from the baking process, which is one of the reasons it is becoming increasingly popular. Because the machine will combine the materials to the appropriate consistency and cook the bread again for an appropriate amount of time, you don't have to worry about over- or under-mixing the ingredients or over- or under-baking the bread.

Buying bread from a store can be more expensive in the long run than using a bread machine, which is another reason to consider investing in one. People with restricted diets or those concerned more about additives and preservatives found in commercial bread will find that using a bread machine allows them more control over the ingredients and the overall quality of the bread they make, which is especially important for those people.

Even though bread machines are simple to operate, there are still certain things you should think about before buying one. Primarily, consider the dimensions of both the machine itself and the loaves it creates. Some machines produce enormous loaves, while others produce smaller ones. Consider how much dough you and your household eat regularly before selecting a machine that can meet your requirements.

Second, take into consideration the functions and software that are available on the device. While some machines come with many customization choices, others are simpler. If you make bread, you can get by with a simple machine. If you have more experience, you should purchase a machine with more options and programs.

Finally, consider how much the machine will cost. The price of a bread machine can range anywhere from several to several hundred dollars. Find out how much money you have available, then hunt for a device that can meet your requirements while staying within your budget.

To summarize, using a bread machine to bake fresh food from scratch is an approach that is not only practical but also economical. Baking Bread may be made simpler and more fun with the assistance of a bread machine, regardless of whether the baker has previous experience or is just starting. You only need to make sure that you give the machine's dimensions, features, and price some thought before making a purchase, and you'll be well on your way to enjoying freshly baked bread every day.

1.1: Brief History of Bread Machines

Late in the 1980s and early the 1990s saw the introduction of the very first bread machines. They were developed to simplify the manufacturing process of manufacturing bread, making it simpler and more practical for anyone to prepare fresh, homemade bread in the comfort of their homes. The early bread machines were relatively straightforward, consisting of little more than a simple clock that enabled users to program when the machine should begin and end its cycle. These early machines underwent a gradual process of evolution that resulted in the addition of more advanced features over time. These new features included various baking cycles, configurable settings, and bigger loaf sizes.

Bread machines have become increasingly popular, leading manufacturers to include additional capabilities in their products. These capabilities include the ability to bake various slices of bread, including gluten-free like whole grain varieties, and select the color of the bread's crust. Many machines could also produce baked goods like jam, pizza dough, and cakes.

By the middle of the 2000s, bread machines became a standard item in many houses, and a broad variety of models were offered to fit a variety of purposes as well as varying levels of spending capacity. Other machines were developed with features that cater to the demands of families and large households, while others were created exclusively for tiny kitchens as they were the target audience for the original design of such machines. Some bread machines also had built-in storage compartments to store utensils and ingredients. This allowed users to make bread more quickly and easily without walking back and forth to the kitchen cupboards to get the necessary items.

In recent years, bread machines have continued to advance, with many versions now integrating cutting-edge features, including voice control, Wi-Fi connectivity, and the ability to integrate with smartphone apps. The modern technology of these machines enables consumers to control the bread maker from virtually any location using their mobile devices, such as smartphones and tablets. In addition, they can be instructed to bake bread for predetermined periods, ensuring that garlic bread is always on hand whenever required.

Some issues exist with bread makers, despite the numerous improvements made to these home gadgets. There have been reports from certain consumers that the bread that is produced by loaf machines tends to be denser and heavier than bread that is traditionally baked and that the exterior may need to be crisper. In addition, there have been reports from some customers that the machines are both noisy and easier to keep clean.

Bread machines continue to be a popular option for many individuals who want to produce fresh bread at home, despite the accusations that have been levelled against them in the past. They provide an easy and effective method of baking bread, during which the user is not required to be present at any point in the baking process, making them quite convenient. A bread machine is an excellent tool to be in your kitchen, whether you are a novice baker or an experienced one. It enables you to make delectable, freshly baked bread whenever you want, and it does so with minimal effort.

Bread machines have a long and interesting history of both innovation and evolution. From their humble origins as simple timer-controlled computers, they have established into sophisticated, high-tech equipment that offers a variety of features and advantages to suit the requirements of various types of users. These appliances have come a long way since their beginnings. A bread machine seems a wonderful option for everyone who enjoys making their fresh bread at home, regardless of whether novice bakers are looking for a quick and simple method to produce fresh bread or more experienced bakers searching for gear that will assist them in creating the ideal loaf.

1.2: Benefits of Using Bread Machines

Bread is a vital food in many households worldwide but baking it from scratch can be time-consuming and labor-intensive. Fortunately, with the invention of bread machines, anyone can

enjoy fresh, homemade bread with minimal effort and time. Now, we will delve into the benefits of using a bread machine and how it can change how you bake at home.

Convenience

One of the main payments of using a bread machine is its convenience. With a bread machine, you can add the ingredients, select the appropriate setting, and let the machine do the rest. You no longer have to spend hours kneading the dough, waiting for it to rise, or shaping it into the desired form. You must add the ingredients, set the timer, and let the machine work magic. This allows you to go about your day without constantly monitoring the bread-making process.

Timesaving

In addition to convenience, using a bread machine also saves you time. The kneading and rising process, which can take hours with traditional methods, is significantly reduced with a bread machine. With a bread machine, you can have a fresh loaf of bread in under an hour, making it a great option for busy individuals and families.

Consistent Results

Another benefit of using a bread machine is that it produces consistent results every time. Unlike traditional methods, where the quality of the bread can vary depending on the strength and experience of the baker, a bread machine ensures that each loaf is baked to perfection. The machine has pre-set settings that control the temperature, timing, and kneading process, making it easy to achieve the desired results every time.

Versatility

Bread machines offer a wide range of versatility, allowing you to bake different types of bread easily. From whole wheat to gluten-free, you can use a bread machine for baking various slices of bread to suit your preferences. Some machines even have specialized settings for baking gluten-free bread, ensuring you can enjoy a delicious loaf even if you have dietary restrictions.

Health Benefits

A bread machine gives you control over the ingredients used in your read. This allows you to use wholesome, nutritious ingredients like whole wheat flour, flax seeds, and oats to make a healthier version of your favorite bread. You can also choose to use organic ingredients or avoid preservatives, providing you with a healthier option than store-bought Bread.

Cost-Effective

While the initial cost may seem high, it can save you money overall. Baking Bread at home is cheaper than buying it from a bakery or store. You can save even more by using readily available ingredients in your pantry.

Easy to Clean

Most bread machines have removable parts, such as the kneading blade and bread pan that can be washed in the dishwasher.

In conclusion, using a bread machine offers numerous benefits that make baking bread at home easier and more convenient. From time-saving to consistent results, versatility, health benefits, cost-effectiveness, and easy cleaning, there are many reasons to invest in a bread machine.

1.3: Essential Ingredients and Equipment

For several reasons, using vital components in a bread maker is crucial. The flavor of the bread is affected by components such as Flour, yeast, salt, Sugar, and fat, which are essential constituents. The flavor of the bread can be altered by altering the amounts of salt and oil and the sort of wheat and sweetener used in the recipe. The bread's texture will be affected in various ways depending on the kinds of flour, wheat, and liquid used. For instance, flour may result in chewy bread, whereas using all flour will produce a loaf of softer bread.

The liquid amount used will also affect the texture of the bread. Using excessive liquid will cause the bread to be dense while using an insufficient amount would result in dry bread. In manufacturing bread, yeast is the most significant leavening agent, and its presence is necessary for the bread to rise. Bread that does not contain yeast will not rise properly and will be heavy and dense. A perfect loaf of bread must have the appropriate proportions for each ingredient. Too much of one component, like yeast, can result in well over and a bitter taste.

On the other hand, not using enough of another ingredient, like salt, might result in bread that lacks flavor. It is necessary to use essential components while making bread in a bread maker to achieve the flavor, texture, seasoning, and balance you seek in the bread. You can bake excellent bread at home that turns out exactly right every time by using the appropriate ingredients and the right quantity of those components.

Flour

Flour is the single most crucial component when it comes to the baking of bread. The flavor and consistency of your bread will be determined, in large part, by the sort of flour you use. Bread flour, all-purpose Flour, whole wheat bread, and gluten-free Flour are typical types of bread.

Yeast

Yeast is the leavening agent responsible for making bread rise when it is baked. Energetic dry yeast and quick yeast are the two available varieties of yeast. Both types of yeast perform equally effectively in a bread machine; however, active dry yeast needs to be stimulated before it can be used, whereas instant fungus can be added straight to the ingredients. Adding salt to the bread improves its flavor and helps control the yeast's activity level.

Sweetener

You can enhance the flavor of bread using sugar, nectar, or other sweets. This also assists the yeast in fermenting properly.

Liquid

Adding liquid, such as milk, milk, or juices, helps moisten the dough and stimulates the yeast. Liquids can be used interchangeably. Adding fat to bread dough, whether in the form of butter, gas or shortening, can enhance the finished product's flavor and texture.

Manufacturing Bread requires some essential equipment, each of which contributes to producing a high-quality loaf. If you don't have the right tools, preparing bread may be a difficult and time-consuming procedure that may produce a loaf that isn't as tasty as it otherwise could have been. A loaf pan, measuring cups & spoons, a kneading blade, and a timer are essential pieces of equipment that play a vital role in the process since they provide accuracy, uniformity, and ease of use. If you have the appropriate tools, you can guarantee that your bread is combined, mashed, and cooked to perfection, resulting in a delicious homemade loaf of bread.

Bread Machine

The bread machine is the most crucial piece of equipment required for making a Bread with the bread machine. Choose a machine that satisfies your requirements, such as the length of the loaf, the kind of bread users want to cook, and any extra features you require in a machine to accomplish this.

Cups and Spoons for Measuring

If you want your bread to turn out well, you need to be able to measure the ingredients accurately. Cups and spoons specifically designed for measuring are required to achieve accurate results.

Bread Pan

In a bread machine, the dough is deposited in the bread pan, referred to as the bread pan. You must select a pizza pan that has a snug fit in your device and is built of a material that is resistant to wear.

Kneading Blade

A kneading blade is a useful tool for mixing and kneading the dough while it is still contained within the bread pan. Some bread makers have a kneading blade that can be removed for more convenient cleaning.

Timer

A timer helps determine when to begin baking bread and guarantees that the bread is cooked for the appropriate length.

To summarize, flour, yeast, salt, a sweetener, liquid, and oil are necessary for making bread in a bread machine. The bread machine, measuring glasses and spoons, a bread pan, a kneading blade, and a timer are all required pieces of equipment for making bread in a bread machine. You will not have any trouble creating fresh bread that tastes great if you have these things.

1.4: Tips for Successful Baking

The use of a bread machine can yield delicious bread if you follow these helpful hints:

1. The secret to producing delicious bread is mastering the precise ingredient measurement. Use measuring utensils like cups and teaspoons to add materials appropriately.

2. A loaf of bread with a superior flavor can be produced using higher-quality ingredients, such as flour that has not been bleached and active dry yeast.

3. The outcomes can vary greatly depending on the type of flour used. Utilize bread flour to achieve a chewy texture. Make use of all-purpose flour to achieve a smoother texture.

4. Warm liquids, as opposed to hot ones, are ideal for yeast growth. To guarantee that the yeast is activated correctly, use liquids with temperatures ranging from 105 to 115 degrees Fahrenheit.

5. The bread maker requires the ingredients to be inserted in a specific order for optimal results. Always make sure to follow the instructions that come with your machine, and always add ingredients inside the order that they are indicated.

6. Depending on the type of loaf you want to make, the settings on your bread machine will be slightly different. To guarantee that you have a successful output, adjust the settings of your bread machine so that they correspond with the sort of dough you are creating.

7. If the bread machine is opened while it is still baking, the loaf of bread may collapse. Hold off on taking the bread out of the machine until it has completed the baking process.

8. To maintain its freshness, bread should be kept in an airtight container. Bread can also be frozen to make it last for a longer period.

1.5: Bread Machine Insights

A bread machine is a compact kitchen equipment specifically developed for baking bread. Because it mixes the ingredients, kneads the dough, lets it rise, and bakes the bread for you, you can produce homemade bread that is both fresh and delicious with extraordinarily little work.

Using a bread machine has several benefits, including the following

Ease of use: all you must do is put in the materials and choose the programmed you want the machine to run. It will take care of everything else. You will save time since the machine will handle the time-consuming chores of mixing, churning, and rising, allowing you to direct your attention to other responsibilities. Every time, the machine's exact timing & temperature control produce bread that is cooked to the same level of perfect bread machines often come with several different settings for different kinds of bread, which enables you to produce a wide range of loaves of bread, such as gluten-free, whole grain, and even cakes & jam.

Some of the drawbacks of using a bread machine are as follows:

- Bread machines are meant for creating tiny loaves, often weighing 1-2 pounds.

- A bread machine is probably not the ideal solution for you if you need to bake bigger loaves because of their limited size.

- Lack of control over the crust: Due to the machine's hermetically sealed environment, there is no way to modify the color of the crust. As a result, the crust may turn out darker or lighter than you would want.

- There is no opportunity to get expertise in hand-kneading the dough. For some individuals, the hands-on experience of kneading & shaping the dough by hand is an integral part of the process of producing bread, and a bread machine eliminates this opportunity.

- A bread machine is a helpful appliance that can make fresh, baked bread with minimum labor. It is particularly helpful for those who are pressed for time or looking for an easy and quick method to bake bread at home.

Chapter 2: Basic Bread Recipes

Bread machines have become commonplace in contemporary kitchens because they make it possible to bake fresh bread in a fraction of the time and effort required by more conventional ways. Before baking bread, you must be familiar with your bread machine's operation. Most bread machines include a pan in the package, and this pan typically has a kneading blade attached to the base of the pan. After the pan has been loaded into the machine, the ingredients are added one at a time in the order that the manufacturer has prescribed. The ability to measure ingredients precisely is essential to producing delicious bread. Ensure that you have a set of measuring cups and spoons to measure the components. Most bread machine recipes require items like flour, yeast, sugar, salt, and water as constituent parts. Selecting the appropriate flour is essential to have a successful experience baking bread. Because bread flour contains more protein than all-purpose flour, it is the type of flour that should be used for baking bread rather than all-purpose flour. Bread flour should always be used whenever a bread machine is involved.

2.1: White Bread

Prep Time: 15 minutes

Cook Time: 240 minutes.

Servings: three

Difficulty level: Medium

Ingredients

- One ½ cup warm water

- Two tablespoons of olive oil

- Two tablespoon butter

- Four cups of bread flour

- One½ teaspoon salt

- Two tablespoons white Sugar

- Two ¼ tsp yeast

Instructions

1. Place the substances in the bread machines in the order they are listed. The ingredients are arranged in a way necessary for the ingredients to go through Cuisinart machines. Check the instruction manual with your product to determine the correct order to add the ingredients. If the order is different, ensure you add them to the order specified in the handbook.

2. Make sure that the basic/white wheat setting is selected. Pick the two-pound loaf size and the color of the crust that you like best.

3. After the final kneading cycle, the kneading paddle should be removed. If you forget this step, extract the paddle from the bread using oven mitts once it has cooled.

4. Once baking, take it out of the bread pan as soon as possible. Before cutting, allow the bread to cool completely on a wire stand for at least 15 to 30 minutes.

Nutrition Facts

Calories: 230, Protein: 10g, Carbs: 45g, Fat: 8g

2.2: Buttery White Bread

Prep Time: 15 minutes

Cook Time: 240 minutes.

Servings: five

Difficulty level: Medium

Ingredients

- 1 1/2 Teaspoons Salt

- 6 Tablespoons Unsalted Butter

- 1 1/2 Teaspoons Bread Machine Yeast

- 1 1/2 Cups Milk

- 4 Cups Bread Flour

- 2 Tablespoons sugar

Instructions

1. Settings for a bread machine include making a loaf of either 1.5 or 2 pounds, with a light color and the "basic" bread setting.

2. Use the microwave to get the butter to a spreadable consistency.

3. Turn off the power to your bread maker.

4. Take on the bread pan out of the dough maker while disconnected.

5. After the milk has been poured into the bread pan, add the remaining ingredients. Put the yeast for the bread machine in last; it should not touch the liquid. Place the bread pan containing the ingredients back into the bread maker while it is unplugged.

6. Turn on the automatic bread machine. Press the "start" button after entering the appropriate settings (for either the 1.5- or 2-pound version of the loaf).

7. Unplug the bread maker and remove the dough pan from the bread machine once the bread has been done baking in the bread maker. Put on oven mitts since the bread pan, and the bread machine will be extremely hot.

8. After removing the bread from the bread pan, set it on and allow it to cool to finish cooling. When withdrawing the bread from the oven, use oven mitts because both the bread and the baking pan will be very hot.

9. You can brush a thin coat of butter here on top of the bread using a pastry brush right after you pull the hot toast from the loaf pan and place it on a cooling rack. To do this, immediately after removing the hot dough from the bread pan, place it on the cooling rack. This results in a crust that is more golden and provides a flavor that is even more buttery. Because when bread is still hot, this method functions most well. Just a heads up: if you use too much-melted butter, it will dip into both sides of the bread and get everywhere. Also, avoid brushing on the topping once the bread has cooled completely.

10. After lifting the bread, you should check to see if the mixing paddle is still embedded in the bread and, if so, remove it. Always protect your hands with oven mitts when handling the mixing paddle after removing it from the bread machine. Alternately, wait till the bread has reached room temperature before removing the mixing paddle from the stand mixer.

11. Before cutting the bread, let it cool for at least an hour and a half on the cooling rack.

12. Please read the advice section below for further information on correctly producing this recipe and avoiding typical problems when using a bread machine.

Nutrition Facts

Calories: 440, Protein: 12g, Carbs: 42g, Fat: 12g

2.3: Thin Sliced White Bread

Prep Time: 30 minutes

Cook Time: 240 minutes.

Servings: five

Difficulty level: Medium

Ingredients

- Two tablespoons of vegetable oil

- One cup water

- One ½ teaspoons salt

- Two teaspoons yeast

- Two tablespoons sugar

- Three ¼ cups flour

Instructions

1. Aerating the flour before measuring it with measuring cups is the correct procedure. Either by sifting the flour through a fine mesh sieve or by aerating it by scrunching it up & whisking it thoroughly, then spooning it into a measuring cup and carefully discarding any excess powder with a knife be accomplished.

2. If you put the measuring cup directly into the bag of sugar and then take some out, you will end up with a significant amount of flour that is more than what is required by the recipe. If you don't aerate the flour, you'll wind up with a dough that's too dry!

3. In the bread machine, combine the water and the oil. Add salt and sugar. Add Flour.

4. Make a shallow depression on the surface of the flour and check to see that it has not reached the liquid ingredients. Put the yeast in the depression that has been made.

5. Separate the yeast and salt as much as possible.

6. Leave the bread pan within the bread machine and press down on it until it snaps into place. Put the cover back on.

7. Select the Basic Bread, 1.5-pound loaf, medium crust, setting on the cycle.

8. After baking, remove your bread pan from the oven while wearing oven mitts. To remove it from the bread pan, turn it upside down and shake it. Allow the loaf to cool on a wire rack for about an hour.

Nutrition Facts

Calories: 230, Protein: 10g, Carbs: 45g, Fat: 8g

2.4: Whole Wheat Bread

Prep Time: 30 minutes

Cook Time: 240 minutes.

Servings: five

Difficulty level: Medium

Ingredients

- One ½ cups water

- One ½ teaspoons salt

- Two tablespoons of melted butter.

- Four cups whole wheat bread flour

- Four teaspoons sugar

- One teaspoon of instant yeast

Instructions

1. This pan of both the bread machine should be layered with the following components in the following manner: milk, butter or oil, salt, sugars, flour, and yeast should be added last.

2. Place the bread pan inside the bread maker and check to see that it is properly fastened. Put the cover back on the machine, and turn it on. Start the machine after selecting the "whole meal" or "whole wheat" bread setting and the "medium" loaf size.

3. Your bread dough will now be kneaded, proofed, and baked by the bread machine on its own without further intervention from you!

4. After the baking cycle has been completed, turn off the power to the bread machine, lift the lid, and take the pan from the appliance while wearing oven mitts. After allowing the loaf to cool for ten minutes inside the pan, remove it

carefully with a shake and let it sit entirely on a wire rack. If the paddle is stuck at the bottom of a loaf, you will need to remove it carefully.

5. It is recommended that all of the components for bread be at room temperature before making the bread. The water temperature must be above 110 degrees Fahrenheit or 45 degrees Celsius to get the yeast to activate.

6. Sifting flour before it is used to make bread helps to aerate the flour, resulting in a lighter and less dense loaf. It is optional for success, but it can be done if one chooses.

7. You will receive a medium loaf that weighs 1 and 12 pounds (750 grams).

8. The number calculated is only a ballpark figure for the lightest loaf if it is cut into 10 slices. This information is specific to each slice.

Nutrition Facts

Calories: 130, Protein: 12g, Carbs: 25g, Fat: 14g

2.5: French bread

Prep Time: 15 minutes

Cook Time: 180 minutes.

Servings: five

Difficulty level: Medium

Ingredients

- 2 tbsps. Sugar

- Four cups of All-purpose Flour

- 1 1/2 tbsps. olive oil

- 1 1/2 tsp. Salt

- 1 1/3 cups Water ; warm

- 2 tsp. Yeast

Instructions

1. Put the water into the bread pan that you have. Check to see that the kneading blade is in the proper position. After that, pour in the sugar, followed by the salt, and finally, the olive oil.

2. Mix in the flour until the liquid is completely covered.

3. Make a shallow depression on the surface of the flour in the middle of the plate, but don't go all the way down to the liquid.

4. Put everything in the bread machine. Put the yeast in this depression and mix it up. (It is essential to add the components in this specific order, especially when using a timer.)

5. Until it is ready to knead the ingredients together, it prevents the yeast from coming into contact with the liquid components of the dough.

6. The yeast will become active far too quickly if liquid substances are used.) At this point, you should prepare the bread machine by inserting the bread pan, setting the timer, and selecting the French Bakery Cycle.

7. This recipe yields a loaf that weighs 2 pounds.

Nutrition Facts

Calories: 120, Protein: 13g, Carbs: 21g, Fat: 9g

2.6: Gluten-Free Bread

Prep Time: 15 minutes

Cook Time: 180 minutes.

Servings: five

Difficulty level: Medium

Ingredients

- One tablespoon sugar

- One tablespoon of dry yeast

- One teaspoon of apple cider vinegar

- Two large eggs

- Two teaspoons of xanthan gum

- One teaspoon salt

- Two ½ cups gluten-free all-purpose baking flour

- One ½ cup warm water

- One ½ tablespoons vegetable oil

Instructions

1. In the order listed, add the following ingredients to a bread machine: water, eggs, oils, vinegar, Bread, xanthan gum, Sugar, salt, and yeast.

2. Start with the Basic cycle in the bread machine, then for the crust, choose either Light or Medium.

3. When the cycle has finished, remove the lid. Please wait until it has cooled before slicing.

4. Put the ingredients into the bread machine in the order specified in the recipe steps, or, if the sequence is different, follow the order that the maker advises of your machine. The instructions provided by the manufacturer could also determine the timing.

Nutrition Facts

Calories: 120, Protein: 13g, Carbs: 21g, Fat: 9g

2.7: **Whole Wheat Bread**

Prep Time: 10 minutes

Cook Time: 150 minutes.

Servings: six

Difficulty level: Easy

Ingredients

- Two cups whole wheat flour

- One cup of all-purpose Flour

- 1/4 cup sugar

- One tablespoon of active dry yeast

- One teaspoon salt

- One cup of warm water

- Two tablespoons of olive oil

Instructions

1. Combine whole wheat flour, most Flour, Sugar, and salt in a large mixing basin and then add them to the bread machine.

2. Combine the hot water, and yeast, with olive oil in a separate basin. 5 minutes should pass for the yeast to activate.

3. When a dough forms, combine the dry components with the moist ones. For 8 to 10 minutes, gently dust a surface and knead the dough.

4. The dough should be placed in a greased basin, covered, and raised for 45 minutes in a warm area.

5. The oven should be heated to 375°F (190°C). 30 to 35 minutes should be used to cook the bread for a beautiful brown crust.

6. Before slicing, take the bread out of the oven and cool it on a cooling rack.

Nutrition Facts

Calories: 190, Protein: 8g, Carbs: 36g, Fat: 5g

Chapter 3: Specialty Bread Recipes

The creativity and understanding of the baker are on display in the form of specialty loaves of bread, each of which is a one-of-a-kind and often complicated recipe. They are produced using a mix of ingredients and processes that set them distinct from regular loaves of bread, making them a wonderful treat for bread lovers and a gorgeous complement to any meal they are served.

3.1: Herb and Cheese Bread

Prep Time: 30 minutes

Cook Time: 40 minutes

Servings: 5

Difficulty level: Easy

Ingredients

- 1 lb. bread flour

- 2 1/4 tsp. instant yeast

- 2 tsp. salt

- 1/4 cup chopped fresh herbs

- 1 tsp. sugar

- 1 cup shredded cheddar cheese

- 1/4 cup olive oil

- 1 1/2 cups warm water

Instructions

1. Add the bread flour, salt, sugar, and yeast to a bread machine until everything is evenly distributed.

2. Blend the olive oil and the warm water in a basin using a whisk.

3. After pouring the liquid components into the dry ingredients, mix everything until it forms a sticky dough.

4. On a surface dusted with flour, knead the dough for eight to ten minutes until it is silky smooth and elastic.

5. Put the dough in an oiled basin, cover it with plastic wrap, and let it rise in a warm location for an hour or until it has doubled in size, whichever comes first.

6. Prepare the oven to 425 degrees Fahrenheit.

7. Grease or line a baking sheet with parchment paper and set it aside.

8. The dough should be rolled out into a broad rectangle approximately half an inch thick.

9. The surface of the dough should be covered with an equal layer of shredded cheese and chopped herbs.

10. Begin at one end of the longer piece of dough and roll it up firmly.

11. On the baking sheet that has been prepared, place the roll with the seam facing down.

12. Bake for 25 to 30 minutes or until the cheese is melted and the bread is golden brown.

13. Wait ten minutes after taking the bread out of the oven before slicing it and serving it.

Nutrition Facts

Calories: 180, Protein: 7g, Carbs: 25g, Fat: 7g

3.2: Fruit and Nut Bread

Prep Time: 15 minutes

Cook Time: 40-45 minutes

Servings: 8-10

Difficulty level: Easy

Ingredients

- 1 lb. bread flour

- 2 1/4 tsp. instant yeast

- 2 tsp. salt

- 1/4 cup chopped fresh herbs (such as basil, thyme, and rosemary)

- 1 tsp. sugar

- 1 cup shredded cheddar cheese

- 1/4 cup olive oil

- 1 1/2 cups warm water

Instructions

1. Turn the temperature on the oven to 350 degrees Fahrenheit (175 degrees Celsius). Prepare a loaf pan that is 9x5 inches and dust it with flour.

2. Add baking powder, flour, baking soda, & salt to the bread machine pan.

3. Sugar, an egg, melted butter, vanilla extract, and yoghurt should be combined in a large dish and beaten with an electric mixer until creamy.

4. Select the "quick bread" or "cake" setting on the bread machine and start the machine.

5. When all the dry ingredients have been added, the wet and dry components should be well-mixed.

6. Blend in the chopped nuts and dried fruits.

7. After the batter has been poured into the prepared loaf pan, the top should be evened out using a spatula.

8. Wait for 40 to 45 mins, or until a toothpick incorporated into the middle of the loaf gets out clean, before taking the loaf out of the oven.

9. After allowing it to cool for ten minutes in the pan, remove the loaf and place it on the wire rack to finish the cooling process.

Nutrition Facts

Calories: 318, Protein: 5g, Carbs: 54g, Fat: 12g

3.3: Braided bread

Prep Time: 1 hour and 30 minutes (including rising time)

Cook Time: 25-30 minutes

Servings: 8-10

Difficulty level: Moderate

Ingredients

- 1 teaspoon salt

- 1 tablespoon unsalted butter, melted

- 2 1/4 teaspoons active dry yeast (1 envelope)

- 1 large egg, beaten

- 3 cups all-purpose Flour

- 1/4 teaspoon granulated sugar

- Sesame or poppy seeds (optional)

- 1/2 cup warm water (105-110°F)

Instructions

1. Add Flour, yeast, salt, and Sugar to the bread machine pan.

2. After adding the warm water to the dry ingredients, whisk everything together until it forms a soft dough.

3. Select the "quick bread" setting on the bread machine and start the machine.

4. After turning the dough onto a surface that has been lightly dusted, knead it for eight to ten minutes or until it is smooth and elastic.

5. Put the dough in an oiled basin, cover it with plastic wrap, and put it in a warm location to rise until it has doubled in size, which should take approximately an hour.

6. Set the temperature in the oven to 375 degrees Fahrenheit (190 degrees Celsius). A baking sheet should be prepared with parchment paper.

7. The dough should be divided into three equal halves. Each part should be rolled into a long, thin rope that is about 12 inches in length.

8. Make a braid out of the ropes, then set the braid on the baking sheet that has been prepared.

9. The braid may be brushed with the beaten egg; if you like, it can be sprinkled with poppy or sesame seeds.

10. Bake for 25 to 30 minutes or until a golden-brown color has developed.

11. The braid should be brushed with melted butter and cooled on a wire rack.

Nutrition Facts

Calories: 138, Protein: 4g, Carbs: 27g, Fat: 3g

3.4: Simple Braided bread

Prep Time: 12-24 hours

Cook Time: 45 minutes

Servings: 8-10 slices

Difficulty level: Intermediate

Ingredients

- 1 cup whole wheat flour

- 2 cups all-purpose Flour

- 1 cup sourdough starter, active and bubbly

- 1 1/2 cups water

- 1 1/2 teaspoons salt

Instructions

1. In a bread machine pan, add Flour, yeast, salt, and Sugar.

2. After adding the warm water to the dry ingredients, whisk everything together until it forms a soft dough.

3. Select the "cake" setting on the bread machine and start the machine.

4. After turning the dough onto a surface that has been lightly dusted, knead it for eight to ten minutes or until it is smooth and elastic.

5. Put the dough in an oiled basin, cover it with plastic wrap, and put it in a warm location to rise until it has doubled in size, which should take approximately an hour.

6. Set the temperature in the oven to 375 degrees Fahrenheit (190 degrees Celsius). A baking sheet should be prepared with parchment paper.

7. The dough should be divided into three equal halves. Each part should be rolled into a long, thin rope that is about 12 inches in length.

8. Make a braid out of the ropes, then set the braid on the baking sheet that has been prepared.

9. The braid may be brushed with the beaten egg; if you like, it can be sprinkled with poppy or sesame seeds.

10. Bake for 25 to 30 minutes or until a golden brown color has developed.

11. The braid should be brushed with melted butter and cooled on a wire rack.

Nutrition Facts

Calories: 143, Protein: 6g, Carbs: 30g, Fat: 1g

3.5: Pumpernickel Bread

Prep Time: 15 minutes

Cook Time: 1 hour and 30 minutes

Servings: 8-10 slices

Difficulty level: Intermediate

Ingredients

- 1/2 cup rye flour

- 2 cups whole wheat flour

- 1 tablespoon caraway seeds (optional)

- 1/2 cup cornmeal

- 1 teaspoon salt

- 1 package (2 1/4 teaspoons) of active dry yeast

- 3 tablespoons molasses

- 2 tablespoons unsalted butter, melted

- 2 tablespoons cocoa powder

- 1 tablespoon instant coffee granules

- 1 cup warm water

- 2 cups all-purpose flour

Instructions

1. Add the yeast, molasses, and warm water to the bread machine pan to make the yeast bread. Allow the mixture to sit undisturbed for five minutes or until it begins to foam.

2. Cocoa powder, instant coffee granules, melted butter, and a pinch of salt should each be combined in their bowl and whisked together.

3. After adding the cocoa mixture, whisk it well to blend it with the yeast mixture.

4. In a separate bowl, combine the whole wheat flour, all-purpose flour, rye flour, cornmeal, and caraway seeds by whisking the ingredients together (if using).

5. Select the "quick bread" or "cake" setting on the bread machine and start the machine.

6. Select the "quick bread" or "cake" setting on the bread machine and start the machine.

7. Add the dry ingredients to the yeast mixture one cup at a time, stirring well after each addition, and do this until all of the dry ingredients have been added.

8. Turn the dough onto a surface dusted with flour, and knead it for five to ten (5-10) minutes or until it is smooth and elastic until has come together.

9. Put the dough in an oiled basin, cover it with plastic wrap, and let it rise in a warm location away from draughts for about an hour or until its size doubles.

10. Prepare your oven by preheating it to 425 degrees Fahrenheit (218 degrees Celsius).

11. Prepare a loaf pan measuring 9 by 5 inches with butter and put it aside.

12. The dough is then pressed down and formed into a loaf. After placing the loaf in the pan that has been prepared, let it rise for an additional twenty minutes.

13. Bake the bread for 1 hour and 15 minutes, or until tapping the bottom of the loaf with your finger produces a hollow sound.

14. Take the bread out of the oven and set it on a wire rack to cool for the remainder of the time.

Nutrition Facts

Calories: 140, Protein: 5g, Carbs: 29g, Fat: 3g

Chapter 4: Dough Recipes

Dough recipes are the base of many wonderful baked items, from bread to pizza. In most cases, they are made of a combination of flour, milk, yeast, salts and a few other components, such as honey and oil. After mixing the ingredients and kneading the dough, it is set to rise so it may be used.

Depending on the desired end product, the resultant dough can be molded into various objects and cooked in the oven, such as loaves, buns, or pizza crusts. Dough recipes come in a wide variety of iterations, including white bread dough, whole wheat bread dough, and pizza dough, all of which have distinctive tastes and textures. Making the dough from home is a fulfilling and satisfying experience since it gives you control over the ingredients and enables you to produce baked delicacies suited to your preference.

4.1: Pizza Dough

Prep Time: 30 minutes

Cook Time: 20 minutes

Servings: 1 medium-sized pizza

Difficulty level: Medium

Ingredients

- 1/4 cup warm water

- 1/2 tablespoon olive oil

- 1/2 teaspoon active dry yeast

- 3/4 to 1 cup all-purpose Flour

- 1/2 teaspoon salt

- 1/2 teaspoon sugar

Instructions

1. In the sequence advised by the manufacturer, add the hot water, sliced olives, salt, sugar, yeast, and wheat flour to a bread maker.

2. Start the machine after selecting the dough setting. The dough will be mixed and kneaded for you by the machine.

3. When the dough is done, please remove it from the machine and place it in a lightly buttered bowl. The bowl should be covered with plastic wrapping and let to rise for 30 to 60 minutes, or until it has doubled in size, in a warm, draft-free environment.

4. Put the dough in a basin that has been lightly greased and cover the bowl with plastic wrap. It should be left to rise in a warm room free from draughts for thirty minutes to one hour or until it has doubled in size.

5. Set the oven temperature to 450 degrees Fahrenheit (230 degrees Celsius).

6. After the dough has had a chance to rise, turn it onto a surface dusted with flour and divide it into four equal pieces. Roll each component into a ball.

7. Each piece of dough should be rolled out into a circle and approximately a quarter of an inch thick. Place the dough in an even layer on a pizza pan and baking sheet that has been lightly oiled.

8. After adding the toppings of your choice, place the pizza into the oven for approximately 10 to 15 minutes, until the dough is browned and the melted cheese has melted, whichever comes first.

9. After removing it from the oven, please wait a few minutes for it to cool down before slicing it up and serving it.

Nutrition Facts

Calories: 220, Protein: 9g, Carbs: 42g, Fat: 5g

4.2: Cinnamon Roll Dough

Prep Time: 30 minutes

Cook Time: 20-25 minutes

Servings: 8-10 rolls

Difficulty level: Medium

Ingredients

- 4 ounces of cream cheese

- 1/3 cup white Sugar

- 1/4 teaspoon ground nutmeg

- 4 cups all-purpose Flour

- 1 cup brown Sugar

- 2 large eggs

- 1 teaspoon salt

- 1 cup powdered Sugar

- 2 tablespoons ground cinnamon

- 2 1/4 teaspoons yeast

- 1 teaspoon vanilla extract

- 1/2 cup unsalted butter

- 1/3 cup unsalted butter

- 1/4 cup unsalted butter

- 1 cup warm milk

- 2 tablespoons warm milk

Instructions

1. In the sequence advised by the manufacturer, add the bacteria, and white sugar, then warm milk in a bread maker.

2. Start the machine after selecting the dough setting. The dough will be mixed and kneaded for you by the machine.

3. The softened butter, egg, pepper, and nutmeg (if using), plus four cups of flour, should then be added to the bread maker after a little while.

4. Once you have a smooth but elastic dough ball, let the machine knead the dough.

5. Remove the dough from the bread maker and place it in a bowl that has been lightly oiled. The bowl should be covered with plastic wrapping and raised for an hour, or until it has doubled in size, in a warm, draft-free environment.

6. Construct the filling by combining a half cup of melted butter, one cup of brown honey, and two tablespoons of cinnamon in a mixing bowl. Do this while your dough is rising.

7. Set the temperature in the oven to 375 degrees Fahrenheit (190 degrees Celsius).

8. When the dough has finished rising, turn it onto a surface dusted with flour and roll it out into a broad rectangle about a quarter of an inch thick. The filling

mixture should be spread over the dough, but a border of about half an inch should be left around the borders.

9. Beginning on one of the longer sides, roll the dough into a log as tightly as possible, beginning at one end. The log should be cut into eight to ten pieces of equal size.

10. Place your cinnamon rolls inside a baking dish 9 inches by 13 inches and oil gently. Bake the rolls for 20 to 25 minutes until they have a golden brown color, and the filling has begun to bubble.

11. Create the frosting in a mixing bowl by combining the creme fraiche, 1/4 cup softened butter, icing sugar, vanilla essence, and warm milk. While the buns are baking, you may make the frosting. The heated rolls should have the icing spread on top of them.

12. Enjoy the cinnamon buns while they are still warm.

Nutrition Facts

Calories: 380, Protein: 6g, Carbs: 63g, Fat: 16g

4.3: Sticky Bun Dough

Prep Time: 30 minutes

Cook Time: 25-30 minutes

Servings: 8-10 buns

Difficulty level: Medium

Ingredients

- 2 large eggs

- 1/2 cup chopped pecans

- 4 cups all-purpose Flour

- 1/2 cup unsalted butter

- 1/2 cup raisins

- 1/4 teaspoon ground cinnamon

- 1 cup brown Sugar

- 1/3 cup white Sugar

- 1 teaspoon salt

- 1 cup warm milk

- 1/3 cup unsalted butter

- 2 1/4 teaspoons yeast

- 1/4 cup heavy cream

Instructions

1. In the order advised by the maker, add the yeast, a fourth cup of white nectar, warm milk, softened butter, egg, 4 pieces of flour, honey, and cinnamon (if used) to the bread maker pan.

2. Click the start button on the bread maker after choosing the dough setting.

3. The machine should be given the recommended time to knead the dough. The precise duration will vary depending on your machine, but it usually takes around 30 minutes.

4. When the dough is done, please remove it from the machine and place it on a flour-dusted surface.

5. The dough should be briefly kneaded on the lightly floured before being placed in a bowl that has been lightly oiled.

6. The dough should rise for an hour, or until it's doubled in size, in a warm, picky environment. Wrap the bowl using plastic wrap.

7. Make your caramel sauce while the bread rises by melting a cup of buttery in a skillet over medium heat. Stir the mixture until the sugars are completely dissolved, and the consistency is uniform after adding 1 cup more brown sugar plus 1/4 cup of creme fraiche. Spread the caramel sauce in a baking dish that is 9 by 13 inches.

8. When the dough has finished rising, turn it onto a surface dusted with flour and roll it out into a broad rectangle about a quarter of an inch thick. On top of the dough, sprinkle the chopped pecans and raisins, if using.

9. Beginning on one of the longer sides, roll the dough into a log as tightly as possible, beginning at one end. The log should be cut into eight to ten pieces of equal size.

10. In the baking tray, arrange the sticky buns so that the cut sides face upward, and then cover them with the caramel sauce. Allow the buns to rise for 20 minutes after covering them with plastic wrap.

11. Set the temperature in the pan to 375 degrees Fahrenheit (190 degrees Celsius).

12. Bake the cinnamon rolls for approximately 25 to 30 minutes until they've become golden brown and the toffee sauce has reached a bubbling state.

13. After letting the buns completely cool for five to ten minutes inside the baking dish, flip them onto a tray ready for serving. Enjoy while it's still warm!

Nutrition Facts

Calories: 380, Protein: 6g, Carbs: 63g, Fat: 16g

4.4: Pretzel Dough

Prep Time: 30 minutes

Cook Time: 12-15 minutes

Servings: 8 pretzels

Difficulty level: Medium

Ingredients

- 5 cups all-purpose Flour

- 1 1/2 cups warm water

- 2 tablespoons brown sugar

- Coarse salt

- 2/3 cup baking soda

- 2 teaspoons salt

- 2 1/4 teaspoons yeast

- 10 cups water

Instructions

1. In the order advised by the manufacturer, add the bread, brown sugar, hot water, and 5 tablespoons of flour, with 2 teaspoons of pepper, to the bread maker pan.

2. Click the start button on the bread maker after choosing the dough setting.

3. The machine should be given the recommended time to knead the dough. The precise duration will vary depending on your machine, but it usually takes around 30 minutes.

4. When the dough is done, please remove it from the machine and place it on a flour-dusted surface.

5. On the floured surface, work the dough over several minutes before placing it in a bowl that has been lightly greased.

6. The dough should rise for an hour or until it's doubled in size in a hot, draft-free environment. Wrap the bowl using plastic wrap.

7. After the dough has had a chance to rise, turn it onto a surface dusted with flour and divide it into eight pieces. Turn each component into a long rope that is rather thin.

8. Make a pretzel out of each rope by constructing a loop with the two ends crossing over one another. To prevent the form from shifting, squeeze the two ends together.

9. Put ten water cups and two-thirds of a cup of sodium bicarbonate into a big saucepan and bring to a boil.

10. Put two or three pretzels into the boiling water for thirty to forty seconds, then remove them using a slotted spoon and set them on a baking sheet that has been lightly oiled.

11. Each pretzel should have some coarse salt sprinkled on top of it.

12. Set the oven temperature to 450 degrees Fahrenheit (230 degrees Celsius).

13. Cook the pretzels in the oven for 12 to 15 minutes until they reach the desired color of golden brown.

14. Warm the pretzels and serve them with cheese dip or mustard, whatever you want.

Nutrition Facts

Calories: 220, Protein: 7g, Carbs: 44g, Fat: 1g

4.5: Bagel Dough

Prep Time: 30 minutes

Cook Time: 12-15 minutes

Servings: 8 bagels

Difficulty level: Medium

Ingredients

- 2 teaspoons salt

- 2 tablespoons sugar

- 2 1/4 teaspoons yeast

- coarse salt

- 1 1/2 cups warm water

- 5 cups all-purpose flour

- Sesame seeds

- 2 tablespoons brown sugar

- 10 cups water

- poppy seeds

Instructions

1. In the sequence recommended by the manufacturer, add the yeast, brown sugar, hot water, 5 cups of wheat, and two tablespoons of salt to the bread maker's pan.

2. Start the machine's dough cycle after choosing it.

3. Verify the consistency of the dough within a few minutes of mixing. Add a spoonful at a time extra flour if it seems too wet. Add a spoonful at a time of more warm water if it seems too dry.

4. Let the dough cycle on the bread maker finish. The bread is ready when the machine beeps or signals.

5. Take the dough from the bread maker and place it lightly dusted with flour on a surface. To form the dough into a ball, knead it for a little while.

6. After the dough has had a chance to rise, turn it into a surface dusted with flour and divide it into eight pieces. Roll each component into a ball.

7. Each ball should have a hole pierced through its middle, and then the rings should be stretched out to make a circle.

8. Bring ten water cups and two teaspoons of sugar to a boil in a big saucepan. Stir occasionally.

9. Put two or three bagels into the simmering solution for one minute, then remove them using a slotted spoon and set them down on a lightly buttered baking sheet.

10. Spread the toppings of your choice evenly across the surface of each bagel.

11. Put the oven to a temperature of 425 degrees Fahrenheit (220 degrees Celsius).

12. Bagels should be baked for 12 to 15 minutes until they reach the desired color of golden brown.

13. Bagels can be served warm with sour cream on the side if preferred.

Nutrition Facts

Calories: 250, Protein: 8g, Carbs: 52g, Fat: 2g

4.6: Dinner Roll Dough

Prep Time: 15 minutes

Cook Time: 15-20 minutes

Servings: 12 dinner rolls

Difficulty level: Easy

Ingredients

- 2 tablespoons melted butter

- 3 cups all-purpose Flour

- 2 tablespoons sugar

- 1 large egg

- 2 1/4 teaspoons yeast

- 1 teaspoon salt

- 1 cup warm milk

Instructions

1. Run the bread maker on a rapid kneading cycle for two to three minutes after adding the milk and the sugar to the pan.

2. Warm milk mixture with yeast added; allow for 5–10 minutes or until foamy.

3. Set the bread maker to the dough setting after adding the flour and salt to the pan.

4. Following the manufacturer's instructions, let the machine knead the dough for the allotted time. When the dough is prepared, please remove it from the bread maker and place it on a floured board.

5. After the dough has had a chance to rise, turn it onto a surface dusted with flour and divide it into 12 pieces. Make a ball out of each of the pieces.

6. Put the dough balls onto a baking dish 9 inches by 13 inches and lightly oil.

7. The egg that has been beaten and the butter that has been melted should be used to glaze the edges of the rolls.

8. Set the temperature in the pan to 375 degrees Fahrenheit (190 degrees Celsius).

9. Bake all rolls for fifteen to twenty minutes or until they become golden brown and make a hollow sound when tapped. Warm the buns and spread butter on them, if desired.

Nutrition Facts

Calories: 120, Protein: 4g, Carbs: 20g, Fat: 4g

Chapter 5: Savory Bread Recipes

Recipes for savory bread are common in many cultures and provide a delicious and satiating choice for various meals and snacks. There are a lot of different kinds of savory bread, each of which has its distinct flavor and texture. These bread can range from crusty bread rolls to soft and fluffy focaccia. The naturally fermented combination of flour, milk and yeast used to make sourdough bread gives it a tangy, tangy taste that goes well with various savory foods. Sourdough Bread is among the most popular savory bread. Ciabatta is another popular type of bread. It is light and airy, and it has a crust that is nice and crunchy. It works well for making Paninis and sandwiches.

A jalapeño cheddar bread, which combines the spiciness of jalapenos with the lusciousness of melted cheddar cheese, maybe the ideal choice for people who want things to get their blood pumping a little bit. A classic French loaf is a terrific alternative if you prefer something slightly more conventional. It has a crunchy exterior and a soft, chewy center, making it ideal for dipping in soups or sauces. Rosemary and garlic toast is a favorite among people who want a more herbaceous taste since the combination of rosemary and garlic produces a mouthwatering perfume and savory and delectable flavor. Focaccia is another choice; it is a light and fluffy bread, traditionally topped with canola oil, salt, and rosemary. As a result, it is an excellent choice for serving with pasta meals or as the foundation for pizzas.

A robust loaf made from whole wheat is an excellent choice for those who want savory bread with more substance. This bread may be used to make sandwiches, toast, or even as a side dish to accompany stew or soup. A multi-grain bread, on the other hand, may provide a combination of tastes and sensations thanks to its assortment of grains, nuts, or seeds, which results in a crust that is nutty and crispy while the center is soft and sensitive. In addition, laver bread can be used as the foundation for other types of meals, such as bruschetta and crostini, in which grilled or toasted bread pieces are layered with a variety of toppings, such as fresh tomatoes and basil, cheese, and cured meats, and then served as an appetizer. These recipes are excellent for freshly and engagingly appreciating savory bread's taste and consistency.

In conclusion, savory bread recipes provide a delectable and adaptable alternative for snacks and meals with a wide selection of possibilities to cater to various preferences and tastes. A savory bread recipe is available that caters to everyone's tastes, whether it be a traditional French baguette, tangy yeast, spicy jalapeño cheddar bread, or something else entirely. Why don't you give one of these mouthwatering loaves a try today and experience the cozy, reassuring flavors of savory bread right in the comfort of your home?

5.1: Garlic Bread

Prep Time: 10 minutes

Cook Time: 15 minutes

Servings: 4-6

Difficulty level: Easy

Ingredients

- 4 cloves of garlic

- 2 tablespoons parsley

- 1/4 cup butter

- 1 teaspoon salt

- 1 loaf of French Bread

- 1/4 cup Parmesan cheese

- 1/4 teaspoon black pepper

Instructions

1. In the mixing bowl of the bread maker, combine the all-purpose wheat, active dry fermentation, salt, sugar, plus garlic powder.

2. Heat the butter and include the minced garlic in a different bowl. Before putting it in the loaf machine's mixing bowl, let it cool a little.

3. The mixing bowl of the bread maker should be filled with warm water.

4. Your bread maker should be set to the "Dough" setting, and you should let it run for 1.5 to 2 hours or until the mixture has tripled in size.

5. When the dough has done proving, take it out of the bread maker and knead it for a few minutes on a floured surface.

6. Prepare your oven by preheating it to 400 degrees Fahrenheit (200 degrees Celsius). Prepare a baking sheet by lining it with parchment paper, then put it to the side.

7. After slicing the slice of bread in halves lengthwise, cut each of those halves into anywhere from four to six equal slices, depending on how large the loaf was.

8. Thoroughly incorporate butter, onion, parsley, salt, and pepper in a low-sided bowl. Use the bowl to stir the ingredients.

9. Spread the cornstarch mixture over both halves of the slices of bread equally using a pastry cutter or your fingertips.

10. If you'd like, sprinkle some grated Parmesan cheese on the bread pieces before serving.

11. After placing the bread pieces on the lined baking sheet, bake them in the oven at the preset temperature for 10 to 15 minutes until the cheese has melted and the bread has a golden-brown crust.

12. Serve the garlic toast while it is still hot, and enjoy it alongside your go-to pasta meal or as a snack.

13. Feel ahead to add more minced garlic to the melted butter if you like the garlicky bread to have a stronger garlic flavor. Alternatively, you might use finely chopped fresh basil for the parsley for a unique taste profile. for a unique taste profile For a unique taste profile For a unique taste profile

Nutrition Facts

Calories: 254, Protein: 5g, Carbs: 28g, Fat: 13g

5.2: Focaccia Bread

Prep Time: 10 minutes

Cook Time: 15 minutes

Servings: 4-6

Difficulty level: Easy

Ingredients

- 2 cups lukewarm water

- 1 to 2 teaspoons rosemary leaves

- 4 cups all-purpose Flour

- 2 teaspoons instant yeast

- boiling water with 1 1/2

- flaky sea salt

- 2 teaspoons kosher salt

- 4 tablespoons olive oil

Instructions

1. To be sure it can manage the quantity of flour or liquid called for in the recipe, check the dough machine's manual. Then, fill the bread device's pan with flour, pepper, and instant yeast.

2. Ensure the recipe's water is at the right temperature before adding it to the pan.

3. Start the cycle after selecting the dough setting on the bread maker. The machine will mix and knead the dough for the allotted period, typically between 10 and 20 minutes.

4. When the dough round is finished, take the dough out and put it in a bowl that has been lightly oiled.

5. The dough should be allowed to rise until it's tripled, which can take anywhere between one and two hours. Cover the container with a moist, damp cloth, bowl cover, or plastic wrap.

6. The dough can be formed and baked following the recipe after it has risen.

7. Flour, salt, and instant yeast should be mixed in a large basin using a whisk. To it, add some water. Mix the ingredients with a rubber spatula until the liquid is completely absorbed and the mixture forms a messy dough ball. Olive oil should be used to coat the surface of the dough delicately. Place the bowl, which has been covered with a moist tea towel, a cloth bowl covering, or plastic wrap, directly into the refrigerator for a minimum of 12 hours and up to three days.

8. The dough must be well-slicked with olive oil, especially if we use a cloth bowl cover or a tea towel as compared to plastic wrap or even a hard lid. This is especially critical if you are going to be storing the dough for an extended period. If you are covering anything with a tea towel, try tying it with an elastic band so it won't let air through. If you do not coat the dough with enough oil, there is a chance that the dough will get dry, and a crust will form on the top layer.

9. You may use parchment paper to line two pie plates of 8 or 9 inches in diameter and a 9 by 13-inch pan, or you can oil it with butter or treat it with non-stick cooking spray.

10. This greasing step may appear unnecessary, yet it is necessary to prevent food from adhering to certain pans.

11. Put one tablespoon of butter in the center of each pan. Using the 9x13-inch pan, put two tablespoons of oil in the center. Deflate your dough by removing it from the edges of the bowl and then dragging it toward the middle of the container while using two forks. As you deflate the bulk into a rough ball, rotate the bowl into quarter turns, so you don't lose your place. With the help of the forks, divide the dough into equal pieces; however, if you use a 9x13-inch pan, you may skip this step.

12. Put one of the pieces of dough into any of the prepared pans, and then roll the dough ball inside the oil to coat it completely and create a rough ball. Proceed in the same manner as the last component. The amount of time they need to rest depends on the temperature in your kitchen and ranges from three to four hours.

13. Put a tray in the center of the oven and turn the temperature to 425 degrees Fahrenheit. If you use rosemary, dot it all over the dough. Each dough circle should have one tablespoon of oil or two teaspoons if you use a 9x13-inch pan. After giving your hands a quick coating of oil by rubbing them together briefly, push firmly down with the tips of your fingers to make deep dimples. If it helps, slightly stretch the material as you create the dimples so that the dough can fill the pan. Salt flakes from the sea should be sprinkled all over the surface.

14. Put the pans or skillet in the oven and cook for 20 to 30 minutes until the bottom is golden brown and crunchy. Take the focaccia out of the oven and place it on a cooling rack once you have removed the pan or pans from the oven. Allow it to cool for at least ten minutes before cutting it and serving it; if you intend to make a sandwich, let it cool fully before halving it.

Nutrition Facts

Calories: 262, Protein: 7g, Carbs: 32g, Fat: 15g

5.3: Onion and Bacon Bread

Prep Time: 10 minutes

Cook Time: 15 minutes

Servings: 16

Difficulty level: Easy

Ingredients

- 3 tablespoons All-Purpose Flour

- 2 teaspoons onion powder

- 2 tablespoons water

- 12 ounces bacon

- 2 tablespoons unsalted butter

- 1/2 cup King Arthur Wheat Flour

- 1 teaspoon paprika

- 1 teaspoon salt

- 3/4 cup lukewarm milk

- 1 1/2 cups onions

- 1/2 teaspoon black pepper

- 1 tablespoon bacon fat

- 2 3/4 cups King Arthur All-Purpose Flour

- 1 large egg

- 2 teaspoons instant yeast

- 1 large egg

Instructions

1. To be sure it can manage the quantity of flour or liquid called for in the recipe, check the dough machine's manual. Then, fill the bread device's pan with flour, pepper, and instant yeast.

2. Ensure the recipe's water is at the right temperature before adding it to the pan.

3. Start the cycle after selecting the dough setting on the bread maker. The machine will mix and knead the dough for the allotted period, typically between 10 and 20 minutes.

4. When the dough round is finished, take the dough out and put it in a bowl that has been lightly oiled.

5. The dough should be allowed to rise until it's tripled, which can take anywhere between one and two hours. Cover the container with a moist, damp cloth, bowl cover, or plastic wrap.

6. The dough can be formed and baked following the recipe after it has risen.

7. Bacon should be cooked until it is crispy and set aside 2 tablespoons of bacon grease before beginning to create the filling.

8. Once the strips have cooled, transfer them to absorbent paper to drain, and then coarsely chop them before placing them in a small bowl.

9. In a large pan over medium-low heat, prepare the onions by cooking them in one tablespoon of the bacon grease that has been retained.

10. Cook the onions over medium heat while tossing them often for ten to fifteen minutes or until they become translucent and start to brown. Take the pan off the heat, then add the chopped onions to the bacon after it has cooled. Mix in the flour, add the pepper and paprika and set the mixture aside.

11. Either weigh your flour or measure it by carefully spooning it into a cup and tapping off any excess with a measuring spoon.

12. Mix the liquid ingredients (milk, water, butter, bacon grease), then add the dry ingredients (Flour, yeast, salt, plus onion powder). After the dough has been mixed and kneaded to the point where it is smooth and pliable, it should be covered and allowed to rise for one hour or until it has doubled.

13. After the first rise, shape the dough into a rectangle about 8 inches by 18 inches. Coat with part of the mixed egg mixture, then spread with bacon filling, reserving 1 tablespoon of the filling for the top "at the point closest to the speaker exposed.

14. While doing so, squeeze the seam together to keep the roll together. Begin rolling the bread from the small side towards the exposed edge.

15. Put the loaf, seam side down, into a 9-by-5-inch pan that has been buttered. Let the dough rise until it becomes dome-shaped, then cover it loosely with oiled plastic wrap and set it aside "to a level over the rim of the pan.

16. Turn the oven temperature to 350 degrees Fahrenheit when the dough starts rising.

Nutrition Facts

Calories: 251, Protein: 11g, Carbs: 25g, Fat: 11g.

5.4: Cheddar and Jalapeno Bread

Prep Time: 10 minutes

Cook Time: 50 minutes

Servings: 8

Difficulty level: Easy

Ingredients

- 2 1/4 tsp instant yeast

- 10 slices jalapeno

- 2 cups warm water

- 3 1/2 cups bread flour

- 1 large jalapeno diced

- 1/3 - 1/2 cup cheddar

- 1 1/2 tsp kosher salt

- 2 cups cheddar cheese

Instructions

1. To be sure it can manage the quantity of flour or liquid called for in the recipe, check the dough machine's manual. Then, fill the bread device's pan with flour, pepper, and instant yeast.

2. Ensure the recipe's water is at the right temperature before adding it to the pan.

3. Start the cycle after selecting the dough setting on the bread maker. The machine will mix and knead the dough for the allotted period, typically between 10 and 20 minutes.

4. When the dough round is finished, take the dough out and put it in a bowl that has been lightly oiled.

5. The dough should be allowed to rise until it's tripled, which can take anywhere between one and two hours. Cover the container with a moist, damp cloth, bowl cover, or plastic wrap.

6. The dough can be formed and baked following the recipe after it has risen. Bread flour, salt, two cups of shredded cheddar cheese, and chopped jalapenos should be added to a medium-sized mixing basin. Mix well, then put aside.

7. Put the yeast and warm water in a large mixing basin (it should be rather big, as the bread will rise in this bowl), and give it a good stir. The water should be hot but not hot (like the temperature of the water used to bathe an infant). After adding the flour mixture to the yeast and water, mix everything with a rubber spatula until there are no more visible streaks of flour.

8. Until you have folded the material in on itself eight to ten times, use a spatula to fold it dough from the edge of the bowl toward the center. Turn the bowl just a little bit each time you fold the dough.

9. Allow rising inside a warm environment for one hour while covered with a towel and uncovered afterwards. After the first hour has passed, take the rubber spatula, and fold the dough into itself eight to ten more times. Allow rising inside a warm location for a further hour while covered with a towel.

10. At the halfway point of this second rise, place your Dutch oven inside the oven with the cover on and preheat the oven to 450 degrees Fahrenheit. Permit it to warm up for the whole half an hour. Place a piece of baking parchment on your work surface that is large enough to line the interior of the Dutch oven and has an overhang. Flour the surface of the counter or chopping board's surface and your hands, and then lightly dust the flour off to a surface that has been dusted with flour. To remove any extra flour, turn the dough over again and brush it off.

11. Until the dough is roughly shaped into a ball, fold the dough's four corners towards the center around six to eight times. Using a piece of parchment paper,

invert the dough to face down. Make cuts in the dough with a sharp knife and do it gently. After giving the dough a brief coating of frying spray (or brushing it with oil), sprinkle it with the 1/3 to 1/2 cup of cheese that was previously put aside and then top it with sliced jalapenos.

12. To safely remove the hot Dutch pot from the oven and the lid, you should wear oven mitts. Using the parchment paper as a guide, carefully move the dough to a Dutch oven. Replace the cover, then go ahead and put it back in the oven. Bake with the cover on for the first 30 minutes of the whole baking time; after that, remove the lid and keep baking for the remaining 20 minutes. After removing the Dutch pan from the oven, please give it a small tilt and then use the paper to pull the bread and paper out of the pot like sliding. It won't be difficult to remove at all.

13. Before slicing the bread, please take off the parchment paper and place it on a wire rack to cool for one to two hours. Before slicing, bread should be completely cooled for the greatest possible texture.

Nutrition Facts

Calories: 371, Protein: 10g, Carbs: 22g, Fat: 12g

5.5: Olive and Rosemary Bread

Prep Time: 10 minutes

Cook Time: 30 minutes

Servings: 8-10

Difficulty level: Medium

Ingredients

- 2 tablespoons fresh rosemary

- 2 tablespoons olive oil

- 1 1/2 cups water

- 5 cups of all-purpose Flour

- 1/2 cup Kalamata olives

- 2 tablespoons sugar

- 1 teaspoon salt

- 2 teaspoons yeast

Instructions

1. To be sure it can manage the quantity of flour or liquid called for in the recipe, check the dough machine's manual. Then, fill the bread device's pan with flour, pepper, and instant yeast.

2. Please ensure the recipe's water is at the right temperature before adding it to the pan.

3. Start the cycle after selecting the dough setting on the bread maker. The machine will mix and knead the dough for the allotted period, typically between 10 and 20 minutes.

4. When the dough round is finished, take the dough out and put it in a bowl that has been lightly oiled.

5. The dough should be allowed to rise until it's tripled, which can take anywhere between one and two hours. Cover the container with a moist, damp cloth, bowl cover, or plastic wrap.

6. The dough can be formed and baked following the recipe after it has risen.

7. On a surface dusted with flour, knead the dough for five to ten minutes, adding additional flour as necessary until the dough appears smooth and elastic.

8. Set the dough inside an oiled basin, cover it with saran wrap, and allow it to rise inside a warm location for an hour or until it has doubled in size, whichever comes first.

9. Prepare your oven by preheating it to 425 degrees Fahrenheit (220 degrees Celsius). Prepare a baking sheet by lining it with parchment paper, then put it to the side.

10. After the dough has had time to rise, punch it back down and knead in the diced veggies and rosemary. Form the mixture into a circular loaf, then set it on the baking sheet previously prepared.

11. Bake the bread in an oven warmed to 350 degrees for thirty minutes or until the crust is light brown and a hollow sound is produced when the bottom of the loaf is tapped.

12. Before slicing or serving the bread, ensure it has had ample time to cool thoroughly on a wire rack.

13. It is recommended to serve this bread warm, and it pairs nicely with a wide variety of spreads, dips, and soups. You may also experiment with other kinds of olives or herbs to see which ones best fit your tastes in terms of flavor. Enjoy!

Nutrition Facts

Calories: 240, Protein: 8g, Carbs: 45g, Fat: 9g.

5.6: Sun-Dried Tomato and Basil Bread

Prep Time: 15 minutes

Cook Time: 25 minutes

Servings: 8

Difficulty level: Easy

Ingredients

- 2 tablespoons fresh basil

- 1/4 cup warm water

- 1/4 cup sun-dried tomatoes

- 2 tablespoons olive oil

- 1/2 teaspoon yeast

- 2 cups of all-purpose Flour

- 1/2 teaspoon sugar

- 1/2 teaspoon salt

Instructions

1. To be sure it can manage the quantity of flour or liquid called for in the recipe, check the dough machine's manual. Then, fill the bread device's pan with flour, pepper, and instant yeast.

2. Ensure the water is at the recipe's right temperature before adding it to the pan.

3. Start the cycle after selecting the dough setting on the bread maker. The machine will mix and knead the dough for the allotted period, typically between 10 and 20 minutes.

4. The sun-dried tomatoes, warm water, olive oil, the basil should all be added now. Combine all the ingredients until you have a sticky ball of dough.

5. When the dough round is finished, take the dough out and put it in a bowl that has been lightly oiled.

6. The dough should be allowed to rise until it's tripled, which can take anywhere between one and two hours. Cover the container with a moist, damp cloth, bowl cover, or plastic wrap.

7. Work the dough for five to seven minutes on a surface dusted with flour or until it is smooth and elastic.

8. Put the dough in a basin that has been buttered, then cover it with plastic wrap. It should be allowed to rise in a warm environment for at least half an hour, but no more than a minute, until it doubles in size.

9. Put the oven to a temperature of 425 degrees Fahrenheit (220 degrees Celsius).

10. Form the mixture into a circular loaf on a surface dusted with flour. Put the dough on the baking tray and give it ten minutes to rest there before continuing.

11. Make slashes on the surface of the dough with a sharp knife in a shallow pattern. Bake the bread for 20 to 25 minutes or until golden brown.

12. Before slicing or serving the bread, let it ten minutes to cool completely first.

Nutrition Facts

Calories: 120, Protein: 4g, Carbs: 20g, Fat: 4g

Chapter 6: Sweet Bread Recipes

The thymus gland & the pancreas both contribute their respective organs to produce sweetbreads. It is likely that since sweetbreads are first soaked in water and then blanched, they do not have the musty odors common in other offal varieties. The taste is not overpowering and has a creamy quality; the consistency is smooth, soft, and moist. The outside may be readily crisped up, and they go well with rich or more acidic sauces.

Although there are too many stages involved in making sweetbreads for them to be a viable option for a midweek supper, they are a pleasant project to take on over the weekend and may be enjoyed with a beautiful bottle of crisp white wine. If you've never had sweetbreads previously, you should take a chance and give them a go. They're delicious!

6.1: Pumpkin Bread

Prep Time: 20 minutes

Cook Time: 60 minutes

Servings: 2

Difficulty level: Medium

Ingredients

- 1 (15-oz) can of 100% pumpkin

- 2 cups Sugar

- ½ teaspoon baking powder

- 2 cups all-purpose Flour

- 2 large eggs

- 1 teaspoon ground nutmeg

- 1 teaspoon baking soda

- 1 teaspoon ground cloves

- 1½ sticks (¾ cup) softened unsalted butter

- ½ teaspoon salt

- 1 teaspoon ground cinnamon

Instructions

1. Put the oven rack in the center point and set the oven's temperature to 325 degrees Fahrenheit. Prepare two loaf pans measuring 8 by 4 inches by liberally greasing them with butter and dusting them with flour. Alternatively, you may use a baking spray containing flour, such as Pam with Flour.

2. In a bread machine pan, flour, baking powder, salt, baking soda, cloves, cinnamon, & nutmeg. Whisk everything together until it is completely incorporated, then put it aside.

3. Cream the sugar and butter in a bread machine until they are completely combined. After each addition of an egg, give the mixture a thorough beating before proceeding. Continue beating for a few more minutes until the mixture is extremely light and fluffy. The pumpkin should be beaten in. It's acceptable if the mixture seems gritty and curdled at this stage; that's just how it should look. Allow the machine to mix and knead the dough.

4. After adding the flour mixture, continue mixing at a moderate speed until everything is incorporated.

5. Bake the cakes for 65–75 minutes, or until a cake sample inserted into the middle of one of the cakes gets out clean. After the batter has been poured into the prepared pans and divided equally, bake the cakes. After allowing the loaves to cool for about ten minutes in the pans, transfer them out onto a cooling rack to finish cooling.

6. The crust on the loaves, which are still warm from the oven, is wonderfully crunchy. If they stay more than a day, you may toast separate slices to achieve the same flavor as when they were just prepared.

7. Freezer-Friendly Bread may be stored in the freezer for up to three months after it has been baked. After reaching its final temperature, package it safely for storage in aluminum foil, freezer wrap, or a freezer bag. Before you serve it, let it thaw in the refrigerator for a whole night.

Nutrition Facts

Calories: 166, Protein: 5g, Carbs: 26g, Fat: 6g

6.2: Lemon Poppy Seed Bread

Prep Time: 15 minutes

Cook Time: 55 minutes

Servings: 1

Difficulty level: Easy

Ingredients

- 1/3 cup (80ml) vegetable oil

- 1/4 teaspoon salt

- 1 Tablespoon lemon zest

- 4 teaspoons poppy seeds

- 2 cups flour (spoon & levelled)

- 1 teaspoon baking soda

- 1 large egg at room temperature

- 1/3 cup (80g) sour cream

- 1/2 teaspoon baking powder

- 2/3 cup (160ml) whole milk

- 3 Tablespoons lemon juice

- 3/4 cup Granulated sugar

Instructions

1. Prepare the oven to 350 degrees Fahrenheit (177 degrees Celsius). Apply non-stick spray to a loaf pan measuring 9 by 5 inches.

2. Put the flour, poppy beans, baking soda, bicarbonate of soda, and salt in a bread machine pan. Egg & granulated sugar should be mixed in a basin of a suitable size until everything is incorporated. Mix the oil, ricotta, milk, lemon juice, & lemon zest into the milk using a whisk. Select the "quick bread" or "cake" setting and start the machine. Once the mixing cycle is complete, pour the batter into a

prepared 9x5 inch loaf pan and bake in a preheated 350-degree Fahrenheit oven for 50 to 60 minutes, covering loosely with foil halfway through.

3. Pour and distribute the batter in an equal layers into the loaf pan that has been prepared. Prepare the bread for 50 to 1 hour, covering the loaf with foil in a loose manner approximately midway through the baking time to ensure that it bakes evenly. Use a toothpick to make a few holes in the bread's middle. If the tester produces no residue, the bread is ready to be consumed. Oven times will differ between ovens. The typical rise time for my Bread is fifty-five minutes.

4. Bread should be allowed to cool in the pan while it is laid on the wire rack.

5. Feel free to sprinkle the bread with the glaze (which will be covered in the following step) while it is still warm. This way, the glaze will soak down into the heated bread, providing even more moisture.

6. This produces a thin coating of glazing rather than a substantial amount. If you want additional glaze, feel free to make two batches. * Combine the lemon juice and confectioner's sugar by whisking them together. Drizzle over the bread while it is still warm in a loaf pan or after it has cooled down completely, whichever comes first.

7. Cut into pieces and serve. Leftover Bread, whether plain or glazed, may be stored at room temperature for up to two days if it is covered or refrigerated for up to a week.

Nutrition Facts

Calories: 140, Protein: 3g, Carbs: 28g, Fat: 3g

6.3: Zucchini Bread

Prep Time: 10 minutes

Cook Time: 50 minutes

Servings: 8-10 slices

Difficulty level: Easy

Ingredients

- 1 teaspoon salt

- 1 teaspoon baking soda

- 2 teaspoons vanilla extract

- 3 eggs

- 1 cup chopped walnuts

- 1 teaspoon cinnamon

- 1 cup vegetable oil

- 1 cup granulated Sugar

- 3 cups all-purpose Flour

- 1 teaspoon baking powder

- 2 cups grated zucchini

Instructions

1. Turn on the oven to 350 °F (175 °C). Grease a 9x5-inch loaf pan.

2. Add the flour, baking soda, baking powder, salt, & cinnamon in a medium basin in a bread machine pan. Turn on the mixing cycle.

3. Beat the eggs, sugar, oil, & vanilla extract until thoroughly combined in a large bowl.

4. Add the grated zucchini and stir.

5. The dry ingredients should be added gradually to the egg mixture & mixed just enough. Avoid overmixing.

6. If using, fold in divided walnuts.

7. Put the prepped loaf pan with the batter inside.

8. 50 to 60 minutes of baking time, or till a toothpick inserted in the middle of the cake comes out clean.

9. Before transferring the bread to cool on a wire rack, let it cool in the pan for 10 minutes.

Nutrition Facts

Calories: 380, Protein: 5g, Carbs: 44g, Fat: 21g

6.4: Banana Bread

Prep Time: 20 minutes

Cook Time: 60 minutes

Servings: 2

Difficulty level: Medium

Ingredients

- 1 teaspoon vanilla extract

- 1/3 cup melted unsalted butter

- 3/4 cup sugar

- 1 teaspoon baking soda

- 1-1/2 cups flour

- 3 ripe bananas, mashed

- 1 large egg, beaten

- 1 teaspoon baking powder

- Pinch of salt

- Optional: 1/2 cup chopped walnuts

Instructions

1. Grease a loaf pan that measures 9x5 inches and preheats the oven to 350°F (175°C).

2. Baking soda, salt, and mashed bananas should all be combined in a bread machine pan.

3. Add sugar, egg, & vanilla extract after thoroughly combining.

4. Start cycle until flour & baking powder are combined.

5. If using, fold in the chopped walnuts.

6. The toothpick inserted in the middle of the loaf should come out clean after 50 minutes of baking. Pour the mixture into the prepared loaf pan.

7. After 10 minutes, remove from the pan and cool on a wire rack.

Nutrition Facts

Calories: 250, Protein: 4g, Carbs: 44g, Fat: 10g

Conclusion

In conclusion, a bread machine is a device that benefits any family because of its adaptability and convenience. At the push of a button, it can produce a variety of loaves of bread, including ones that do not contain gluten and those made with whole wheat. Before making a purchase, it is essential to consider various aspects, including the available settings, the available configurations, and the additional features, due to the wide variety of options currently on the market.

Not only does using a bread machine reduce the amount of time and effort required, but it also results from an inherent that is consistently delicious. The user can concentrate on other activities because the machine handles the kneading, rising, and baking on their behalf. In addition, if you want to save money on bread but don't want to buy it from the store, using a bread machine to make it rather than buying it, there is an excellent way to do so. When you use a bread machine, you can experiment with various ingredients and methods for making bread. To make pieces of bread that are one of a kind and delicious, you may customize them by including a variety of spices, fruits, nuts, and even veggies. You can even choose the crust color and texture to suit your preferences using the machine's various settings, giving you much control over the process.

On the other hand, you must be aware that a bread machine is not a magical piece of equipment that can consistently produce excellent bread. For it to perform successfully, it requires correct use and regular maintenance, just like any other item in the kitchen. Adhering to the manufacturer's directions and recommendations is critical for the greatest possible outcomes. In conclusion, a bread machine is an appliance every home baker should have in their kitchen. It is an investment that is well worth it because of its adaptability, convenience, and capacity to produce delicious fresh bread. A bread machine is a fantastic tool to have in the kitchen, regardless of whether you are an experienced baker or are just beginning your journey in the world of baking. Consequently, if you want to save time and effort while still appreciating the delectable flavor of freshly made bread, you should seriously consider purchasing a bread machine as soon as possible.

Manufactured by Amazon.ca
Bolton, ON

33369740R00046